National Novel Writing Month's Young Novelist Workbook

Middle School
Fourth Edition

Created by National Novel Writing Month

Table of Contents

Hello, Novelist!

Here it is, almost November, and you've decided to join over 100,000 people around the world next month who are brave and crazy enough to write a novel in 30 days.

We know what you're thinking. You're thinking: Writing a novel sounds pretty cool. After all, when I'm done I can spend the rest of my life bragging about how I wrote a novel in a month. But still, isn't novel writing for, well, novelists?

The answer, our friends, is no! Anyone can write a novel. You don't even have to know how to write a novel to write a novel. You just have to have a few ideas, some paper, and a pen. It's as easy as that.

If you don't have any ideas about what to write next month, don't worry. We've put together this workbook to spark your imagination before NaNoWriMo. We'll walk you through creating awesome characters and settings. We'll show you how to create conflict, outline your plot, and write dialogue that will strike the deepest envy in writers the world over. Then, as if that wasn't enough, we will be right by your side throughout NaNoWriMo with exercises that will help you boost your word count, create plot twists, and get to know your characters better than you might want to.

Before you embark on your noveling adventure, we want you to know that whatever your word count at the end of November, you are extraordinary just for giving this a shot.

Good luck, from all of us here at NaNoWriMo. May your words be many, your imagination be awakened, and your adventure be out of this world!

Novel Writing How-Tos

Inner Editor Containment Button

Before you begin your month-long noveling adventure, you'll want to do away with your Inner Editor. What is your Inner Editor? He's the nagging, no-fun beast we bring along with us on all our creative endeavors. He sits on our shoulder and points out our typos and misspellings and every awkward sentence. When he's in a particularly nasty mood, he might try to tell us that we're embarrassingly awful writers, and shouldn't even be allowed to put pen to paper. He is helpful to have around when taking tests and revising things we've already written (and any other things where we're shooting for perfection). But he'll slow you down in the worst way if you let him write your novel with you next month.

No matter how ridiculous this might sound, close your eyes and imagine your Inner Editor. Think about what he or she might look like. Is your Inner Editor a man or a woman? Is he or she holding a dictionary? Chasing after you with a ruler? Once you get a good picture in your head of what he or she looks like, open your eyes and push the button below.

Warning: Pushing the button will vacuum your Inner Editor right out of your head for the next 30 days. He'll be transported from your brain into a NaNoWriMo Inner Editor Containment Cell, where we'll put him to use proofreading our Young Writers Program websites. We have lots for him to do! And we promise that after 30 days we'll give him back to you (so you'll have him around to help out with your novel rewrites).

Congratulations. Your Inner Editor has been successfully contained. It's time to move on.

What Makes a Novel a Novel?

Now that you've received the scary news that you're going to write a novel, you're probably wondering exactly what that means. You may have guessed that a novel is a book with a story in it. But what makes a novel different from, say, that picture book you loved as a kindergartener? Or an unauthorized biography of the tallest man on Earth?

> A **novel** is a long book that tells a story of made-up characters and events. It is written in prose and contains a conflict, or problem, that the characters try to solve.

If you're not sure what "prose" means, that's just a fancy word for writing that sounds like normal speech instead of poetry.

Think of books you've read recently. Which were novels? Which weren't? **Choose one of those books, preferably one that you really like a lot or just know inside and out. Write the name of that book and its author here:**

My Novel Model or My Model Novel:

_____

by _____

For the rest of your novel-writing adventure, think of that book as a model you can use when you get stuck. You don't have to imitate it—and you never want to copy it, of course—but you can always look at it for ideas. Just think of that novel's author as your own personal novel-writing coach.

Now take out your model novel and fill in the blanks below.

1. Who are the most important characters in your model novel?

_____

_____

2. Which character do you think is the most important? Why?

_____

_____

_____

3. What is the book mostly about? What is the central conflict?

_____

_____

_____

_____

4. Whose perspective is the novel written from (as in, who is telling the story)? How do you know?

_____

_____

5. This means that the novel is written in (check one of the following):

☐ First person. (One of the characters tells the story using the word "I".)

☐ Third person. (The story is not told by a character. No "I" is used.)

☐ Second person. (The story is addressed to "you." This is very rare!)

☐ Multiple perspectives. (More than one of the above is used.)

6. How does the novel begin?

_____

_____

7. Where and when does it take place, generally?

_____

8. What is your favorite thing about this novel?

_____

_____

_____

Now that you've explored how and why your novel makes a good model, you're ready to present it to classmates with a book talk. Don't worry; a book talk is not a book report. You don't have to describe everything that happens in the book in excruciating detail. Instead, a book talk is like an advertisement for the book, or a movie trailer.

Your job is to give your audience just enough information to want to wrestle that book out of your hands and read it themselves. Take a look at this book talk, for example, about the real novel *When You Reach Me* by Rebecca Stead.

> Have you ever wondered what it would be like to know what's going to happen in the future? Well, what if somebody else could tell you, but only communicated by sending mysterious messages? In *When You Reach Me* by Rebecca Stead, 12-year-old Miranda starts finding notes about events in her future—that end up coming true! All of a sudden Miranda's life is turned upside down: her mom's apartment key is stolen, her best friend Sal will no longer talk to her, and the anonymous notes start hinting that something dangerous is about to happen. Miranda realizes that she may be the only one able to prevent a tragedy, and maybe even change the future.

After reading this book talk, you know the basics of *When You Reach Me*: its title, its author, its main character, and some important things happening in the main character's life. But you probably have a bunch of questions, too. How is Miranda getting the messages? Are they really warnings from the future, or is something else going on? Why did her best friend stop talking to her? Perhaps you are curious enough to check out this book for yourself!

As you can see, a book talk simply gives the audience a "taste" of what the book is about and who its main characters are

Below, prepare your own book talk about the novel you chose as your model. And remember, a little enthusiasm goes a long way!

_____

_____

_____

_____

_____

_____

_____

_____

_____

Good Book, Bad Book

Out of all the books you've read so far in your life, there were those that were ridiculously fun to read and some that were just about as fun as visiting the dentist on your birthday. Before you start thinking about the novel you'll be writing this November, it's helpful to write down what, to you, makes a book "good" (interesting, exciting, and fun to read) and what makes a book "bad" (boring, totally unbelievable, painful to read, etc.).

Good Book

Let's start by making a list of books you love. Think about all the novels you've read that you couldn't put down no matter how tired you were or how much unfinished homework was piling up all around you. **In the spaces below, write down the title and author of three books you love:**

1. Title _____

   Author _____

2. Title _____

   Author _____

3. Title _____

   Author _____

Now, make a list of everything you can think of that made those books so amazing. What made the characters so fascinating? What made the story events somehow believable, even if they could never happen in real life? You can be as general or as detailed as you like; include anything from "adventurous characters" to "high school drama" to "witty and natural dialogue."

_____

_____

_____

_____

_____

_____

_____

_____

_____

Once you have finished this list, keep it with you at all times during November. Why is this list so important? Because, as you might imagine, the things you like as a reader are going to be things you are best at writing. As you write your story, refer to this list of ingredients, and consider adding them to your novel when you're stuck for ideas or directions.

Bad Book

Now, think about all those books you've read or started to read that put you to sleep by the end of page one. You know, the ones that you'd rather eat a mayonnaise, peanut butter, and onion sandwich than have to read again. **In the spaces below, list the title and author of three books you really did not like reading.**

1. Title _____

   Author _____

2. Title   _____

   Author   _____

3. Title   _____

   Author   _____

Now, write a list of things that, to you, made these books so awful. Were the characters or events just too far-fetched? Did you think to yourself "I could *totally* have done a better job than these authors"? Again, you can be as general or as detailed as you like; include anything from "cheesy endings" to "unbelievable plot twists."

_____

_____

_____

_____

_____

_____

_____

_____

_____

Just like the list of things you love in a book, keep this list with you at all times during November. It might seem strange that you would have to remind yourself of the things you dislike in novels, but these items are experts in the art of ending up in your story without you even realizing it.

Creating Interesting Characters

Some people think that an exciting plot is all it takes to make a story good, but in order to have an exciting plot, you need interesting, complex characters.

Boring Characters vs. Interesting Characters

Boring Character: Luna lives in Philidelphia.

Interesting Character: 15-year-old Luna just moved from her childhood home in California to Philadelphia. She is having a really hard time making friends at school. Her strange name and the beat-up, psychedelic-colored van her dad drives her to school in every morning have not made it easy on her.

To make matters even worse, the girls are jealous of the attention she gets from guys because of her wild green eyes, dark tan, and cool California accent.

They are also jealous of her shoes.

She has every shoe known to man. Colorful sandals, hip skate shoes, cute high heels, wedges, boots, tennis shoes, running shoes—she wears a new pair each day. Little do they know, she makes them all herself.

Not only are characters with hidden depths and secrets more fun to read about, they're also more fun to write about! Though you'll end up writing about a bunch of different people in your novel next month, all of them will fall into one of three categories: **The protagonist, the supporting characters,** and **the antagonist.**

The Protagonist
The **protagonist** is the character with the starring role in your book. In most novels, the protagonist is on a journey to get what he or she wants more than anything else in the world, whether it's fame, or revenge, or something as simple as joining the high school football team.

The Supporting Characters
Supporting characters are characters who help the protagonist achieve his or her goal. Many novels have several supporting characters, including your protagonist's family members, friends, neighbors, helpful wise old gurus, you name it. These characters also have dreams of their own, and their adventures will add even more excitement to your novel.

The Antagonist

The antagonist is the character in a novel that is standing in the way of the protagonist achieving his or her goal. That does not mean that all antagonists are evil, scheming monsters. Some antagonists stand in the way simply through jealousy, or misunderstanding, or by having a set of goals that differs from the protagonist's. If Fernando is your protagonist and he wants to take Jill to the dance, but Greg asked her first, this doesn't mean Greg is a "bad guy." He's just another guy who likes the same girl. Then again, there are those antagonists that are just plain evil. It's up to you to decide who's going to stand in your protagonist's way, and how he or she is going to do it.

It's a great idea for you, the author, to try and get to know your characters before you begin writing. We asked a team of scientists, mathematicians, and creative writing gurus from around the world: "What's the easiest way for a writer to get to know their characters?" Hands down, they all agreed the single best way is to **fill out a Character Questionnaire for all your characters.**

Go ahead and fill out the following questionnaire for your protagonist, antagonist, and for as many supporting characters as you'd like.

Character Questionnaire

Section One: All Your Characters
Complete Section One for every character in your book.

Section Two: Questions for Your Supporting Characters
Complete Section Two just for your supporting characters.

Section Three: Questions for Your Antagonist
Complete Section Three just for your antagonist.

Section Four: Bonus Questions!
Complete Section Four if you want to get to know all your characters even better. Remember, the more you know about your characters, the easier it will be to bring them to life on the page!

Section One: Complete this section for all your characters!

1. Name:

2. Age:

3. Height:

4. Eye color:

5. Physical appearance:

6. Unique physical attributes:

7. Hobbies/interests:

8. Where does he or she live? What is it like there?

9. Special skills/abilities:

10. Family (describe):

11. Description of his or her house:

12. Description of his or her bedroom:

13. Favorite bands/songs/type of music:

14. Favorite movies:

15. Favorite TV shows:

16. Favorite books:

17. Favorite foods:

18. Favorite sports/sports teams:

19. Political views:

20. Any interesting philosophies on life?

21. Religion:

22. Physical health:

23. Pet peeves:

Section Two: Supporting Character Questions

1. Relationship to the protagonist:

2. Favorite thing about the protagonist:

3. Similarities to protagonist:

4. Differences from protagonist:

Section Three: Antagonist Questions

1. Why is he or she facing off against the protagonist?

2. Any likeable traits?

3. Sure-fire ways to defeat your antagonist:

Section Four: Bonus Questions!

1. Favorite clothing style/outfit:

2. Special gestures/movements (i.e., curling his/her lip when speaking, always keeping his/her eyes on the ground, etc.):

3. Things about his/her appearance he/she would most like to change:

4. Speaking style (fast, talkative, monotone, etc.):

5. Fondest memory:

6. Insecurities:

7. Quirks:

8. Temperament (easygoing, easily angered, etc.):

9. Negative traits:

10. Things that upset him or her:

11. Things that embarrass him or her:

12. This character really cares about:

10. Things that make him or her happy:

11. Deepest, darkest secret:

12. Reason he or she kept this secret for so long:

13. Other people's opinions of this character (What do people like about this character? What do they dislike about this character?):

14. Dream vacation:

15. Any pets?

16. Best thing that has ever happened to this character:

17. Worst thing that has ever happened to this character:

18. Superstitions:

19. Three words to describe this character:

20. If a song played every time this character walked into the room, what song would it be?

Creating Conflict

Ok, so you know who your characters are. Excellent. Now it is time to figure out what your characters are going to do this November. **Most stories are ultimately about the same thing—the journey a protagonist goes on to get what he or she wants.** Whether the goal is to become the next "American Idol" or to discover the cure for cancer, his or her journey is never easy, and your character will encounter many setbacks along the way. Though they're no fun for your protagonist, these obstacles are what make your story exciting to read.

Imagine a story about someone named Jim who wants a sandwich more than anything in the world. How boring would the story be if all Jim had to do was walk from his bedroom to the kitchen and eat a sandwich? That story is so uneventful it can be told in one sentence. But what if Jim is seriously afraid of the dark, the power is out in his house, and he has to walk down a dark hallway to get to the kitchen? And, once there, he has to fight his cruel older sister, Helga, for the last two pieces of bread?

That story has both external conflict and internal conflict.

External Conflict
The external conflict is the one between a protagonist and antagonist. In the above story, the protagonist (Jim) has a goal (to eat a sandwich), but a motivated antagonist (Helga) has his or her own agendas (to also eat a sandwich). The struggle between Jim and Helga over the last two pieces of bread is the external conflict in this story.

Internal Conflict
The internal conflicts are the fears and insecurities that a protagonist has to overcome in order to get what he or she wants. In the story above, Jim has to overcome his fear of the dark in order to get the sandwich he wants so badly.

If you have completed your character questionnaires, you already know a good amount about the major players in your novel. Now it's time to answer some deeper questions about your characters' hopes and fears in order to create the conflicts that will make your novel interesting.

Take out and review your character questionnaires, then fill in the blanks below.

Your Protagonist

More than anything in the world, my protagonist wants:

_____

_____

_____

_____

_____

But he/she is afraid of:

_____

_____

_____

_____

_____

And his/her greatest weakness is (is it something like Kryptonite or more like Hostess snack cakes?):

_____

_____

_____

_____

_____

Not to mention that no-good antagonist . . .

Your Antagonist

More than anything in the world, my antagonist wants (this can be as simple as defeating the protagonist or something more ambitious like world domination):

_____

_____

_____

_____

_____

_____

My antagonist's "beef" with the protagonist is:

_____

_____

_____

_____

_____

_____

My antagonist is afraid of (kittens?):

_____

_____

_____

_____

_____

_____

His/her greatest weakness is:

_____

_____

_____

_____

_____

_____

Congratulations! You now have the basic ingredients for a juicy story: **external conflict and internal conflict.** Know that your internal and external conflicts will overlap throughout your novel. Once your characters find out about each others' fears and weaknesses, you better believe they will use them against each other mercilessly as they fight to make their own dreams come true.

Outlining Your Plot

Now that you've created some exciting conflict for your novel, you probably have an idea of what is going to happen in your book this November. You may know what kind of journey your protagonist will undertake, and you know what will stand in his or her way. Now it's time to take the next step and map out how everything is going to happen.

Writing an entire novel from beginning to end may seem impossible, but once you have a plan, it is not as hard as you think. Trust us. Most stories have the same structure, and break down into the same six sections that make up a plot. See the diagram below.

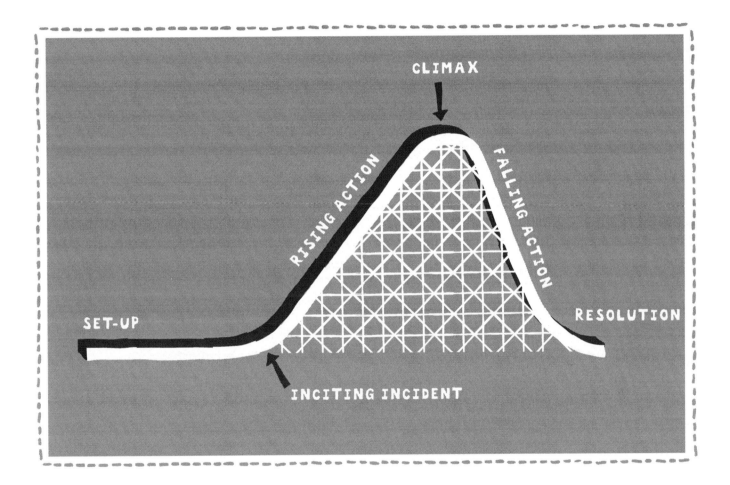

This diagram may look familiar to you. It is most commonly in the shape of an inverted checkmark, but we think a plot rollercoaster sounds much more fun than a checkmark, so we're going with that.

Even if this is stuff you already know from English class, carefully read all the sections below before you move on to map out your own plot.

The Set-Up

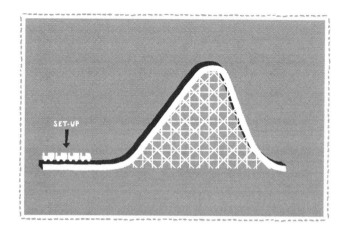

What kind of rollercoaster are we getting on?

Though some novels begin with an "inciting incident"—which you will read about in just a second—many of them start by telling the reader a little bit about the characters, the setting, and the conflict before jumping into the action. Just like you'd want to know what kind of rollercoaster you're getting on before waiting in line, a reader wants to know what kind of novel he or she is about to read before committing time to it.

Here is an example of a story's set-up:

Boris is in his bedroom playing guitar and eating frosted strawberry Pop-Tarts. His hot-pink Mohawk bobs up and down as he plays and jumps from side to side. He knocks over his Coke by mistake, adding to the litter on the floor in his messy room. His walls are covered with rock posters, and his floor is covered with guitar magazines and how-to books, pedals, and various cords and connectors.

His mom, Wilma, walks into his room with a plate of Pop-Tarts. She dodges him as he swings his guitar behind his back, and continues to play.

"Showoff," Wilma says playfully.

"Mom, I'm so over it!" Boris shouts over his amp.

Wilma turns his amp off. "Over what?" she says. "What does that even mean?"

"I am bored with everything." Boris pushes some dirty clothes off his bed and sits down.

"I don't understand you at all, little man," Wilma says, handing Boris the plate of pastries. "You have every guitar and guitar gadget in the world. What else do you need?"

"How many times do I have to tell you to stop calling me 'little man'?

"I'm way too old to be sitting in my bedroom like a loser." Boris shoves a Pop-Tart in his mouth and talks with his mouth full. "I want to be in a band. I want to travel the world . . ."

"I've been telling you, you should check out that new reality TV show, *So You Think You Can Rock?*! I hear auditions are coming to Detroit next weekend, and the grand prize is a $2,000,000 contract with Capitol Records."

"Yeah right!" Boris says. "I'd pass out cold in front of an audience that big. And that judge, Billy Van Carnage, is a total jerk. I get nervous even thinking about him."

Okay, that was a good set up. We have been introduced to the protagonist and story's main conflicts: Boris wants to join a rock band and travel the world, but he has crippling stage fright (internal conflict). Plus, it has been hinted that Mr. Van Carnage is also going to pose a problem for Boris (external conflict).

The Inciting Incident

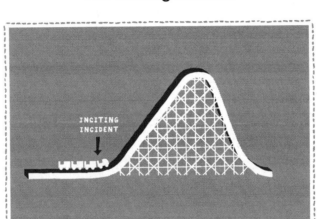

Getting On the Rollercoaster

The inciting incident launches your protagonist into the adventure whether he or she is ready or not. It can be a pretty scary moment for your main character. Once it happens, there's no turning back.

Here is the inciting incident that happens in this story:

Boris is looking at a bright pink Stratocaster when he sees Abigail at the counter. Afraid of saying something stupid to her, he ducks behind a drum set, but it's too late. He's been spotted.

Abigail walks over and picks up the guitar Boris was just looking at. "Look—it matches your hair perfectly. You have to get it."

"Yeah. Sounds like a plan." Boris' face is slowly turning a shade of pink that matches his hair.

Abigail doesn't seem to notice. "So guess what?" she asks.

"Um...nothing," Boris stammers. "I mean, I'm great!...I mean, what?"

Abigail laughs. "My band is trying out for *So You Think You Can Rock?* this weekend."

"Wow, you're so cool," Boris says. "I mean, that's so cool. What is your band called?"

"Crude Medicine," Abigail says, looking a little nervous herself. "I'm glad I ran into you. I've heard you're a pretty awesome lead guitarist and our guy is M.I.A. We're starting to freak out."

She pauses and looks around, then looks back at Boris. "If he doesn't show, would you fill in for the tryout?"

"Um, wow, um, wow. . ." A bead of sweat runs down Boris' forehead.

"I'll take that as a 'yes'!" Abigail hugs Boris, catching him totally off guard.

"I'll be at your place at 8 AM sharp Saturday morning. Make sure you know the guitar solo in this song by then." Abigail hands Boris a burned CD and runs out the door.

If an inciting incident never happened, Boris would more than likely continue to eat breakfast pastries and play guitar alone in his bedroom. This might sound like a pretty fun life to live, but it is not a very fun life to read about.

Rising Action

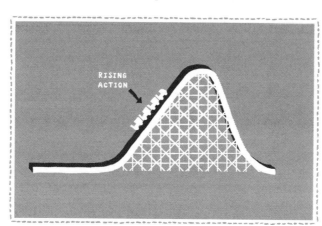

Climbing the Big Hill

This will be the longest section of your novel. You will develop your characters, deepen their relationships with one another, and lay out everything that happens to them before the **climax**. Think of the rising action as the biggest hill on the rollercoaster—the higher you go, the more suspenseful it gets. The rising action is made up of many events, each of them building to the most exciting part of your story: the climax.

Here is a summary of some of the rising action in this story:

1. Abigail pulls up outside in her beat-up Volkswagen Jetta and Boris–trying not to look back to his room where his guitars, amps, and pedals are looking sad and deserted–says goodbye to his mom

Abigail honks until Boris finally hugs his mom, grabs his vintage Fender Jaguar and runs out the door.

2.   As soon as they get to the auditions, Boris starts to get nervous. He can barely talk to people, but Abigail and the other two band members, Zach (the drummer) and Megan (the bassist), do all the talking. Though Boris is nervous about getting on stage, he finds himself becoming more and more comfortable around Abigail. She is unlike any other girl he has ever met. And she seems to like him.

3.   When it's time for Crude Medicine to get up in front of the judges to play, Boris can hardly see straight. Boris knows the song like the back of his hand, so all he has to worry about is not throwing up or passing out.
Boris makes it all the way through the song just fine, and Abigail sings lead and nails it. All the judges are blown away, except one.

"Girl lead singers are cliché," Billy Van Carnage says, and then points at Boris. "And I'm pretty sure that this guy will lose his lunch on stage opening night, and that would not be pretty."
But the rest of the judges outvote him. Crude Medicine is on its way to stardom.

4. Crude Medicine makes it all the way to the final episode and each performance gets easier for Boris. Boris figures they are going to win, and spends less time worrying about impressing the judges and more time daydreaming about all the ways to spend his part of the prize money—a six-month tropical vacation with Abigail, a new house for his mom, or maybe a large donation to a local music school for urban kids. Losing, at this point, is not an option.

The Climax

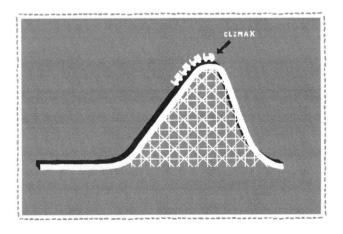

The Top of the Rollercoaster

This is the "gasp" moment. This is the moment at the very top of the rollercoaster, right before your high-speed drop. This moment doesn't last long, and neither does the climax in your novel. It can be as short as one paragraph—just enough to make your readers hold their breath in suspense and ask, "What's going to happen next?!"

Here is an example of a climax:

The members of Crude Medicine take the stage in their new bright orange jumpsuits and white sunglasses. The audience cheers. Boris and Abigail wave to the crowd, and then Zach counts them in with a few clicks of his drumsticks As soon as Boris hits the first note on his guitar they know that something is terribly wrong. His guitar sounds like 100 sick cats crying, and the bass doesn't sound much better.

Abigail begins to sing, but her voice sounds horrible. Even the microphone is out of tune. The band members all look around with expressions of total disbelief. An empty Coke can is thrown at Abigail, and the audience starts booing until the show cuts to commercial break.

The Falling Action

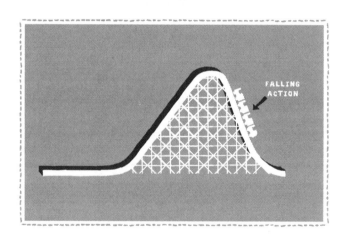

The High-Speed Drop

The falling action is what happens next. It is the fast-paced, action-packed part of your novel. You're finally speeding down the tracks of the rollercoaster with your hands in the air! Does the antagonist get defeated? Do the protagonist's dreams finally come true? If so, how?

Here is an example of falling action:

Crude Medicine, humiliated, exits stage right. None of them speak, but they all shoot suspicious glances at one another while the judges make their final decision.

"It's just so strange," Gill says. "They were doing so well."

"I told you chicks can't rock," Billy says, but before he can say another word the stage manager runs out to the judges' table with a tape. Kendra pops it in the instant replay player and, lo and behold, it shows Billy messing with the band's equipment before the show.

"I never . . ." Billy begins, but it is too late. Two beefy security guards carry him away.

Gill gets up on stage and the show goes live again.

"Sorry about that everyone, looks like Billy Van Carnage messed with Crude Medicine's equipment before they went on, so I would like to invite them back up for an encore."

The band plays, and there is no doubt in anyone's mind that they are the winners of *So You Think You Can Rock!?* 2008.

The Resolution

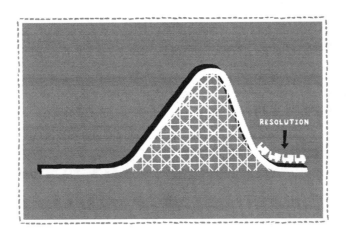

Getting Off the Rollercoaster

This is how things work out in the very end, after your protagonist gets (or doesn't get) what he or she wants. It has been said by creative writing sages that your characters—especially your protagonist—must change over the course of the book. This change happens little by little as your character battles his or her fears, defeats villains, and builds friendships and relationships with a cast of amazing characters. All of these adventures will end up changing the way your main character sees the world and his or her place in it. Try to use the final scenes to highlight those changes.

An example of a resolution:

Crude Medicine is playing an arena full of rabid fans.

"Hello Detroit!" Boris yells. "It's good to be home!"

He walks over to Abigail, and they high five, then kiss, and the crowd screams.

"Let's rock!" Abigail says.

The band plays, the crowd sings, and Boris looks just as comfortable on stage now as he did less than one year ago rocking out alone in his bedroom.

Now it's your turn to create your plot. Believe us, if you fill out this worksheet, noveling will be ten times easier in November. You don't have to describe everything that will happen in your novel here. This is just to help you get an idea about what'll happen in the beginning, middle, and end of your book.

1. Describe Your Set-Up

In one to two paragraphs, describe a scene that introduces your characters, your setting, and the main conflicts in your story. You may want to review your Conflict Worksheet before you do this.

2. Describe Your Inciting Incident

In one paragraph, describe the event that causes your protagonist to begin his or her adventure.

3. Describe Some of Your Rising Action:

Write a list of five events that build up to the climax of your novel. Don't forget to include all of your supporting characters!

4. Describe Your Climax:

In one paragraph, describe what will happen in the climax of your novel.

5. Describe Your Falling Action:

In one to two paragraphs, describe what happens after the climax. Does your protagonist get what he or she wants? Does the antagonist get defeated? How?

6. Describe Your Resolution:

In one to two paragraphs, describe how everything works out in the very end. Is it a happy ending? Sad? Remember to show how your characters changed because of their journey.

After you've finished your plot outline, you can take it one step further and fill out the blank "Plot Rollercoaster" on Page 29. To get an idea of how to use the blank rollercoaster, check out the example we've created on the next page.

Example Plot Rollercoaster

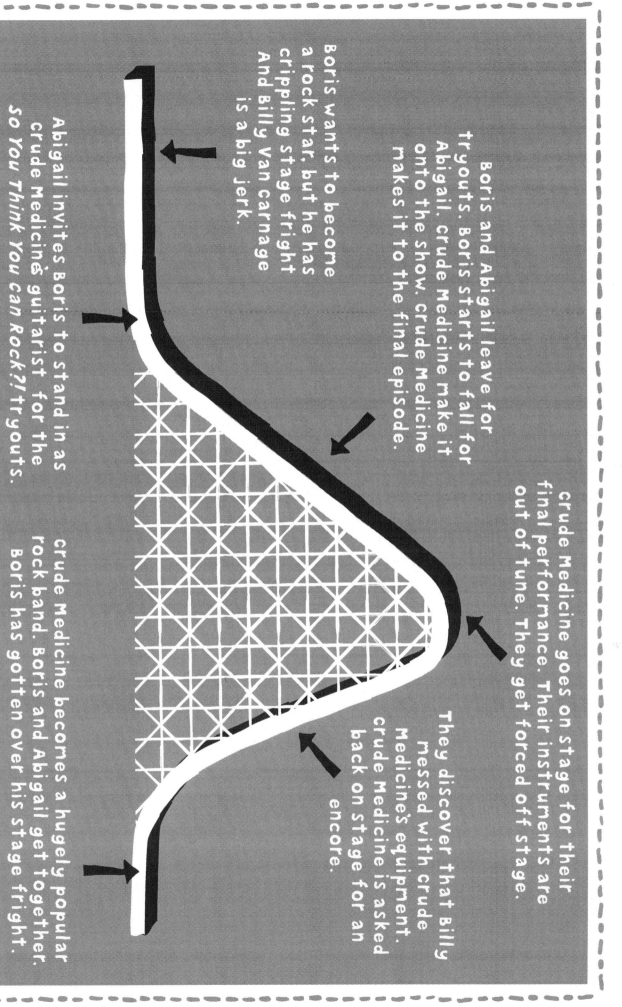

Boris and Abigail leave for tryouts. Boris starts to fall for Abigail. crude Medicine make it onto the show. crude Medicine makes it to the final episode.

Boris wants to become a rock star, but he has crippling stage fright And Billy van carnage is a big jerk.

Abigail invites Boris to stand in as crude Medicine's guitarist for the show. so You Think You can Rock?! tryouts.

crude Medicine becomes a hugely popular rock band. Boris and Abigail get together. Boris has gotten over his stage fright.

crude Medicine goes on stage for their final performance. Their instruments are out of tune. They get forced off stage.

They discover that Billy messed with crude Medicine's equipment. crude Medicine is asked back on stage for an encore.

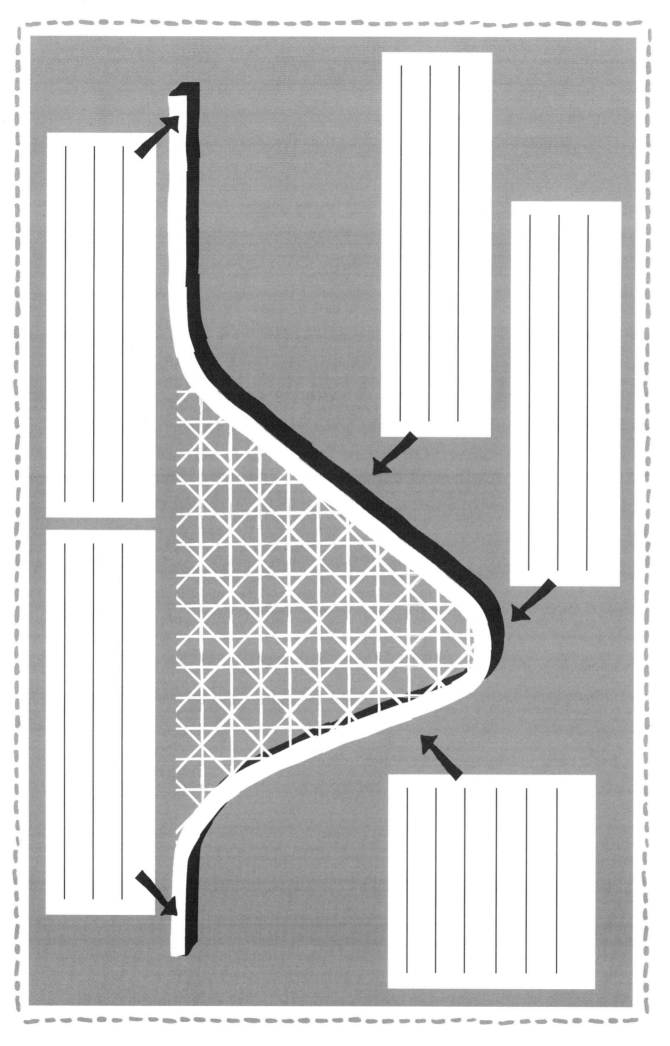

Plot Rollercoaster

29

FINAL NOTE ON PLOT!

As you probably know, not all rollercoasters have the same track. They all have different hills and drops, different speeds, different twists and turns, and loops and tunnels. The same goes for novels. That is what makes them different and exciting. Sometimes they begin with the inciting incident or work backwards from the resolution to the beginning. Novels are filled with flashbacks, flash-forwards, and unexpected plot twists. And novels don't have to have happy endings either. Just like life, sometimes things don't work out exactly the way you planned them to. In November, experiment with the plot you create by thinking beyond the "typical one-hill rollercoaster" formula. Rearrange events, add some twists, and flip that resolution on its head. You'll be surprised at how much this can energize your story.

Setting

Setting and Mood

Now that you have a good idea of what the plot of your novel is going to be, it's time to really nail down some of the settings for your novel. The setting of a novel is where and when the story takes place. As you know, most novels have more than one setting. Usually, the author decides to have one large setting (like a certain town in the 18th century), and then many smaller settings (like the Laundromat where the characters hang out on the weekends). But settings do more than serve as a backdrop to the action in your novel. Your settings can also add to the mood of your novel.

A **mood** describes the emotional quality of something, whether it is a song, a painting, or, in this case, a scene in your novel. It might help to think of mood as the way you want someone to feel while reading your novel.

If you wanted to create a creepy mood for a scene in your novel, you could start with something like:

"A one-eyed crow is picking at something on a branch of a dead tree in the yard, while a three-legged dog howls at the moon."

These images remind us of dark, disturbing things, and show the reader that the scene of the novel is "creepy" without having to tell him or her directly.

For each of the moods listed below, write some details about a setting that would help create that mood. Try to write two or three sentences for each mood. Don't forget to use a lot of details as you write.

Sad

_____

_____

_____

_____

_____

Celebratory/happy

_____

_____

_____

_____

_____

Suspenseful

_____

_____

_____

_____

_____

Now make up three of your own "moods" and describe a setting that would go along with each one.

_____

_____

_____

_____

_____

_____

_____

_____

_____

_____

_____

_____

_____

_____

The last step is to apply your new skills to your upcoming novel. For those of you who mapped out your plot using the previous worksheet, take it out. For the following plot points, describe a setting that would fit the mood of your scene.

Set-up

_____

_____

_____

_____

_____

Inciting incident

_____

_____

_____

_____

_____

A selected scene from your rising action

_____

_____

_____

_____

_____

The climax

_____

_____

_____

_____

_____

A selected scene from your falling action

_____

_____

_____

_____

_____

Resolution

_____

_____

_____

_____

_____

Great! Now you have settings that enhance the different moods that are in your novel-to-be. You may want to keep this page handy and use it as you write your novel next month.

Bonus Setting Exercises: Settings that Reinforce Characters

Another great, sophisticated writing trick is to use setting to reinforce your characters. For example, if you are writing about a mysterious person, you might place him or her in a dark mansion on a hill outside of town. Or, if one of your characters is feeling trapped in his or her life, they might live in a small town in the middle of nowhere.

Here's us just telling you about Larry:
Larry was having a hard time. He felt sad and trapped. He was once a famous author, but he hadn't written a word for years.

And here's us telling you about Larry, but through the space that he is living in:
Larry's apartment was less of a living space than a glorified closet. The bathroom was just big enough to sit on the toilet without having his knees touch the sink, and the window was more like a ship's porthole. The bed was so small his feet hung over the edge, and there was really not much to do but watch static on the television.

The place did not have a kitchen, so he bought a camping hotplate to make his single-serving meals. He ate the same thing every night, but like a house cat, he did not seem to mind the monotony of his repeated dinner of rice, wilted spinach, and baked beans.

Nothing hung on the walls of Larry's place, but old framed photos of family members he no longer spoke to cluttered his small desk. An old dusty typewriter and a stack of blank paper took up the rest of the space there.

He hadn't written a word in years.

Larry doesn't even have to speak for himself; his apartment speaks for him!

For each of the following characters, try to come up with a setting that will reflect or reinforce what you imagine about them. As you write, try to be as detailed as possible. Don't forget colors, sounds, and even smells.

The shy new girl in town

_____

_____

_____

_____

_____

A criminal on the run

_____

_____

_____

_____

_____

A rebellious teen with nothing to lose

_____

_____

_____

_____

_____

Your protagonist

_____

_____

_____

_____

Your antagonist

_____

_____

_____

_____

_____

(Supporting character's name)

_____

_____

_____

_____

_____

(Supporting character's name)

_____

_____

_____

_____

_____

(Supporting character's name)

_____

_____

_____

_____

_____

Awesome. Not only do you have _mood_ enhancing settings for your novel, you also have _character_ enhancing settings. Again, before you move on and forget all about all the amazing settings you just created, keep this page close at hand so in November you can access it easily.

Writing Really Good Dialogue

Dialogue is what happens when two or more characters speak to one another. We experience dialogue all the time in our everyday lives.

Here's some dialogue you might have heard today:

"Hey, dude. How are you?"
"I'm really good. Thanks for asking. And you?"
"Good, thanks."

Of course, this kind of dialogue is important. If we didn't say hello and ask people how they are doing, we might lose a lot of friends, fast. But in a novel, long scenes of this kind of daily dialogue end up being boring. Readers want to experience something outside of their everyday experience. They want to hear characters make interesting or exciting declarations, or challenge each other, or reveal the whereabouts of hidden treasure.

Dialogue in a novel should do one, if not all, of the following:

1. Move the story forward
2. Increase the tension
3. Help to define characters

Here's a couple of example exchanges to illustrate each:

> **Dialogue that moves your story forward:**
>
> The phone rang, and Jerry picked it up. "Hello?"
> There was a moment of silence on the other end, then, "Jerry? Is this Jerry Simmons?"
> "Yes. Who's this?" Jerry asked.
> "Jerry..." The other man paused. Jerry could hear him take a deep breath. "Jerry, my name is Dave. I'm your brother."
> "I don't have a brother." Jerry said, losing his patience. "My family died years ago."
> "Not your whole family," Dave said.

Right away, we want to know who this Dave fellow is, if he's telling the truth, and how he found Jerry. Basically, we want to know what will happen next. In fact, this is a great inciting incident. The discovery of a long-lost sibling is certain to move your story forward in interesting ways.

> **Dialogue that increases the tension:**
>
> "Dave!" Jerry shouted. "We've got to get away from here! The building's gonna blow!"
> "We've got to go back!" Dave screamed.
> "Why?"
> Dave pointed at the roof. "Because Susan's still up there!"

Talk about tense. Are Dave and Jerry going to save Susan? It's a matter of life and death here, and this little exchange of dialogue has us wanting more.

"Dude, totally!"

In your own novel, you might think about the ways an accent, some slang, or funny quirks of speech can really work to enhance and define your characters. A character that says "Shiver me timbers!" all the time is certainly a different person than a character that says "Dude, totally!")

Dialogue Tags Other Than "Said":

acknowledged
admitted
agreed
answered
argued
asked
barked
begged
bellowed
blustered
bragged
complained
confessed
cried
demanded
denied

Dialogue that defines characters:

"What up, G-dawg?" Mark said. "You got a table for one? I'm starved!"

The waiter looked up to see Mark. "Good morning to you, young man. Welcome to our fine establishment."

"I've been playing *Rock Band* for 40 hours straight! I need like ten sandwiches!" Mark exclaimed.

"I am so sorry, but I am going to have to ask you to keep your voice down if we are to provide you with the ten sandwiches you requested," Greg said.

giggled
hinted
hissed
howled
interrupted
laughed
lied
mumbled
muttered
nagged
pleaded
promised
questioned
remembered
replied
requested
roared
sang
screamed
screeched
shouted
sighed
snarled
sobbed
threatened
warned
whimpered
whined
whispered
wondered
yelled

Obviously, Mark and the waiter are two very different people, and we can tell this just by the way they talk. It's likely that Mark is much younger than the waiter, and he is clearly more hip and excitable. The waiter, on the other hand, is more formal, and doesn't know the first thing about youth culture. He hasn't even heard of *Rock Band*. In just a few seconds of dialogue, the audience finds out a lot about these characters and how they relate to one another.

Comic Strip Exercise

Writing good dialogue is like writing a comic strip. Comic artists only have so many boxes to fill before they run out of room. If they spend too much time on "Hey, dude, how are you?" pretty soon, they've run out of boxes. To help you understand how boring this kind of dialogue can be, we've put together a nifty example of a Boring Comic Strip. Check it out!

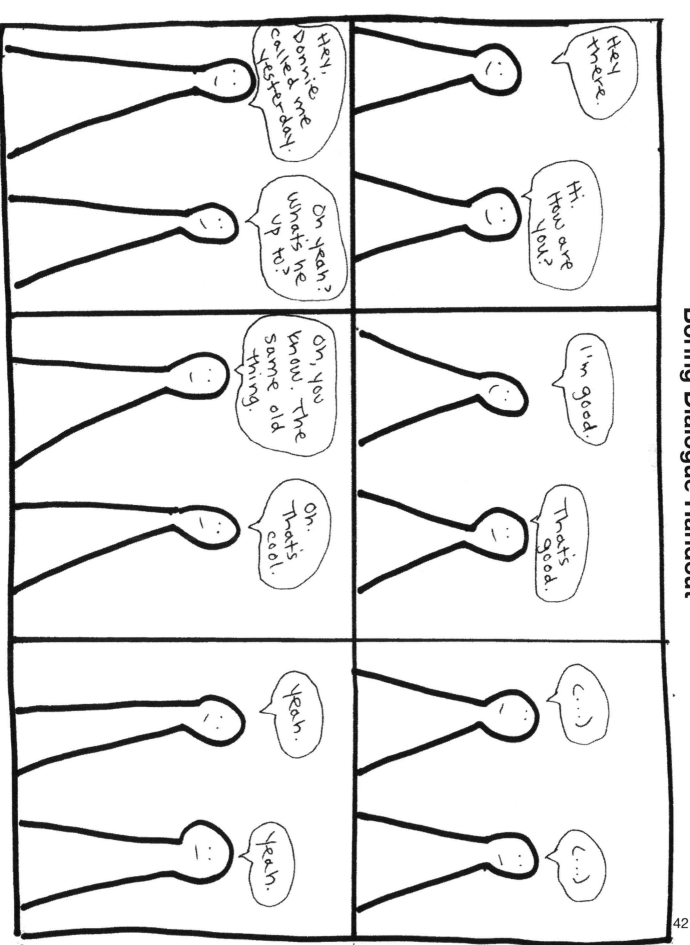

Fill in the following three Blank Comic Strips. You can include any of the characters you've created for your novel in these comics.

1. In the first comic, write a scene from your novel that moves the story forward.
2. In the second one, try to write dialogue that increases the tension.
3. In the final one, write a conversation that helps the reader better understand your characters.

Remember, though, that you've only got six boxes to use in each, so you need to say a lot—that is, your characters need to say a lot—in a small space. It's a challenge, but we know you're up to it. Later, if you like what you've written, you can plop this dialogue right into your novel using quotation marks.

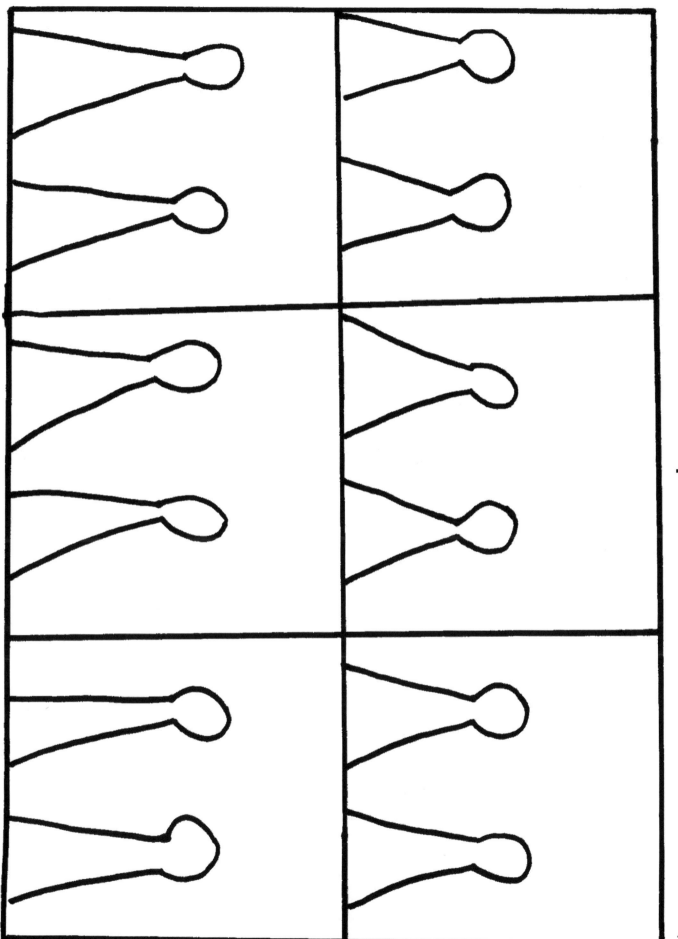

45

Comic Strip Worksheet

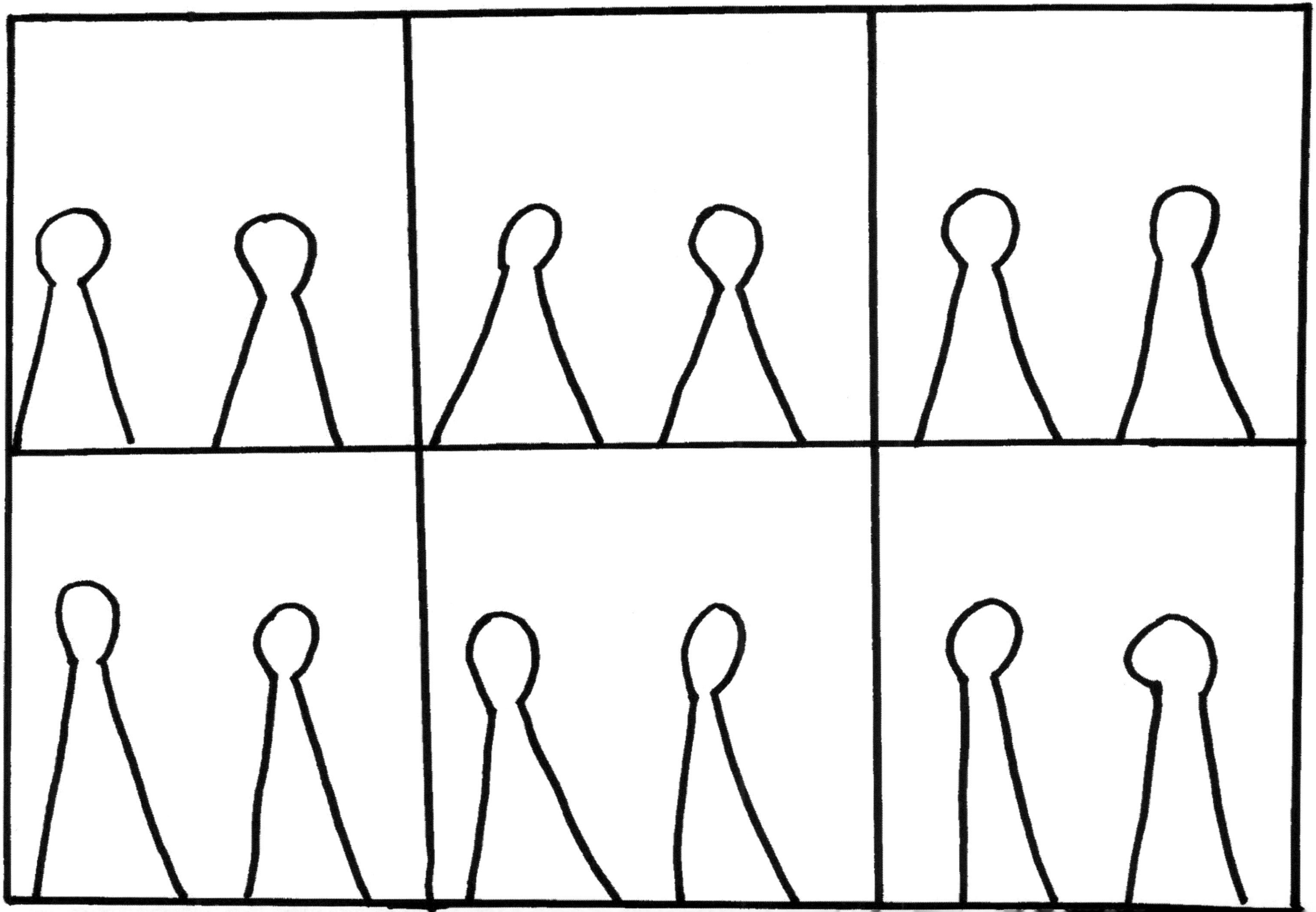

Getting Ready for NaNoWriMo

NaNoWriMo Survival Tips

Now that you know how to write a novel, you may be wondering how you write a novel in a month. We've put together a few ideas to help you get ready for your noveling adventure. First we would like share with you our **Top Five NaNoWriMo Survival Tips:**

5. **Reward yourself.** Make sure you do really nice things for yourself all throughout November. Every time you reach a word-count milestone, give yourself a reward! Eat cookies for lunch, drink soda for breakfast, or call all your friends and brag about how many words you've written so far.

4. **Keep moving.** Get out of that chair and stretch your arms and legs. Do a couple of sit-ups or jumping jacks. Challenge your next-door neighbor to an arm-wrestling competition! Keeping your blood moving will keep the ideas flowing.

3. **Get plenty of sleep.** Just because you're writing a novel in a month doesn't mean you should neglect sleep. Besides, you never know what kind of interesting characters and settings your dreams might reveal.

2. **Borrow from your everyday life.** It is totally okay to borrow material from your life, and the lives around you. Professional novelists do this all the time, even if they don't admit it. In fact, writing about your life is a great idea if this is your first novel. Just remember to change the names before you let your friends read it!

1. **Never say you "can't."** This is the most important thing to remember next month! There are no can'ts in month-long novel writing.

You can do it.

Remember that tens of thousands of people just like you write a novel in a month every year. No matter how busy you are, or how little you might know about writing a novel, you can finish! If you begin the month thinking you *can*, you are already way ahead of the game.

National Novel Writing Month Contract

This is an agreement that lays out your rights and responsibilities as a novelist. Make sure that both you and a reliable teacher, parent, or friend sign this contract. Once this affidavit is signed, the contract will broadcast your novel-writing intentions throughout the universe. Really.

NATIONAL NOVEL WRITING MONTH

CONTRACT

I, _____ , hereby pledge my intent to write a

_____ -word novel in one month.

By taking on this absurd month-long deadline, I understand that notions of craft, brilliance, grammar, and spelling are to be chucked right out the window, where they will remain, ignored, until they are retrieved for the editing process. I understand that I am a talented person, capable of heroic acts of creativity, and I will give myself enough time over the course of the next month to allow my innate gifts to come to the surface, untouched by self-doubt, self-criticism, and other acts of self-bullying.

During the month ahead, I realize I will produce clunky dialogue, clichéd characters, and deeply flawed plots. I agree that all of these things will be left in my rough draft, to be corrected at a later point. I understand my right to withhold my manuscript from all readers (except possibly my teacher) until I deem it complete. I also acknowledge my right as an author to brag about the quality of the rough draft and the rigors of the writing process, should such bragging prove useful in garnering me respect, attention, or freedom from household chores.

I acknowledge that the month-long, _____ - word deadline I set for myself is absolute and unchangeable, and that any failure to meet the deadline, or any effort on my part to move the deadline once the adventure has begun, will result in well-deserved mockery from friends and family. I also acknowledge that, upon successful completion of the stated writing objective, I am entitled to a period of gleeful celebration and revelry lasting days, if not weeks, afterward.

_____   _____
YOUR SIGNATURE   DATE

_____   _____
TEACHER/PARENT/RELIABLE FRIEND'S SIGNATURE   DATE

Word-Count Chore Coupons

If you feel like you need more motivation to meet your word-count goal, promise to do unpleasant chores for your family members, teachers, and even your best friends. Below you will find ten chore coupons, one for each milestone that you will find on your Triumphant Chart of Noveling Progress on page 55. If you vow to clean out your little sister's rat cage if you don't make your first word-count milestone, you better believe you'll make your word count! Get a pair of scissors, cut these out, and give them to people you know.

NANOWRIMO YWP — **CHORE COUPONS**

I _____
YOUR NAME

hereby promise to render _____
CHORE

_____

unto _____
RECIPIENTS NAME

should I fail to write _____
AMOUNT

words of my novel by _____
DATE

X _____
SIGNED   DATE

NANOWRIMO YWP — **CHORE COUPONS**

I _____
YOUR NAME

hereby promise to render _____
CHORE

_____

unto _____
RECIPIENTS NAME

should I fail to write _____
AMOUNT

words of my novel by _____
DATE

X _____
SIGNED   DATE

NANOWRIMO YWP — **CHORE COUPONS**

I _____
YOUR NAME

hereby promise to render _____
CHORE

_____

unto _____
RECIPIENTS NAME

should I fail to write _____
AMOUNT

words of my novel by _____
DATE

X _____
SIGNED   DATE

NANOWRIMO YWP — **CHORE COUPONS**

I _____
YOUR NAME

hereby promise to render _____
CHORE

_____

unto _____
RECIPIENTS NAME

should I fail to write _____
AMOUNT

words of my novel by _____
DATE

X _____
SIGNED   DATE

NANOWRIMO YWP — CHORE COUPONS

I _____
YOUR NAME
hereby promise to render _____
CHORE
_____
unto _____
RECIPIENTS NAME
should I fail to write _____
AMOUNT
words of my novel by _____
DATE

X
SIGNED   DATE

NANOWRIMO YWP — CHORE COUPONS

I _____
YOUR NAME
hereby promise to render _____
CHORE
_____
unto _____
RECIPIENTS NAME
should I fail to write _____
AMOUNT
words of my novel by _____
DATE

X
SIGNED   DATE

NANOWRIMO YWP — CHORE COUPONS

I _____
YOUR NAME
hereby promise to render _____
CHORE
_____
unto _____
RECIPIENTS NAME
should I fail to write _____
AMOUNT
words of my novel by _____
DATE

X
SIGNED   DATE

NANOWRIMO YWP — CHORE COUPONS

I _____
YOUR NAME
hereby promise to render _____
CHORE
_____
unto _____
RECIPIENTS NAME
should I fail to write _____
AMOUNT
words of my novel by _____
DATE

X
SIGNED   DATE

NANOWRIMO YWP — CHORE COUPONS

I _____
YOUR NAME
hereby promise to render _____
CHORE
_____
unto _____
RECIPIENTS NAME
should I fail to write _____
AMOUNT
words of my novel by _____
DATE

X
SIGNED   DATE

NANOWRIMO YWP — CHORE COUPONS

I _____
YOUR NAME
hereby promise to render _____
CHORE
_____
unto _____
RECIPIENTS NAME
should I fail to write _____
AMOUNT
words of my novel by _____
DATE

X
SIGNED   DATE

NaNoWriMo Calendar

Your word-count goal for the month may seem impossible from where you're sitting now. That's totally okay. Big creative projects like novel writing are daunting even for professional writers, but we're here to tell you a secret: **If you break big goals into a series of smaller goals, the impossible becomes doable. Easy, even.** To help make next month's challenge a piece of cake, we've come up with this NaNoWriMo Calendar.

It is best to set aside time each day to write, but be realistic. If you can only write three days a week because you have soccer practice, be make sure to take that into consideration when filling in this calendar. Jot down the number of hours and words you plan on writing each day.

Tip: If you want to find out just how many words you will need to write each day, divide your total word-count by the number of days you've set aside for writing during the month. For example, if your word-count goal is 5,000, and you can make time to write on 20 days, you will need to write 250 words each day you've scheduled.)

1
I will write from
_____ TIME
_____ AM/PM
to
_____ TIME
_____ AM/PM
Word-count goal for the day
_____ AMOUNT

2
I will write from
_____ TIME
_____ AM/PM
to
_____ TIME
_____ AM/PM
Word-count goal for the day
_____ AMOUNT

3
I will write from
_____ TIME
_____ AM/PM
to
_____ TIME
_____ AM/PM
Word-count goal for the day
_____ AMOUNT

4
I will write from
_____ TIME
_____ AM/PM
to
_____ TIME
_____ AM/PM
Word-count goal for the day
_____ AMOUNT

5
I will write from
_____ TIME
_____ AM/PM
to
_____ TIME
_____ AM/PM
Word-count goal for the day
_____ AMOUNT

6
I will write from
_____ TIME
_____ AM/PM
to
_____ TIME
_____ AM/PM
Word-count goal for the day
_____ AMOUNT

7
I will write from
_____ TIME
_____ AM/PM
to
_____ TIME
_____ AM/PM
Word-count goal for the day
_____ AMOUNT

8
I will write from
_____ TIME
_____ AM/PM
to
_____ TIME
_____ AM/PM
Word-count goal for the day
_____ AMOUNT

9
I will write from
_____ TIME
_____ AM/PM
to
_____ TIME
_____ AM/PM
Word-count goal for the day
_____ AMOUNT

10
I will write from
_____ TIME
_____ AM/PM
to
_____ TIME
_____ AM/PM
Word-count goal for the day
_____ AMOUNT

11
I will write from
_____ TIME
_____ AM/PM
to
_____ TIME
_____ AM/PM
Word-count goal for the day
_____ AMOUNT

12
I will write from
_____ TIME
_____ AM/PM
to
_____ TIME
_____ AM/PM
Word-count goal for the day
_____ AMOUNT

13
I will write from
_____ TIME
_____ AM/PM
to
_____ TIME
_____ AM/PM
Word-count goal for the day
_____ AMOUNT

14
I will write from
_____ TIME
_____ AM/PM
to
_____ TIME
_____ AM/PM
Word-count goal for the day
_____ AMOUNT

15
I will write from
_____ TIME
_____ AM/PM
to
_____ TIME
_____ AM/PM
Word-count goal for the day
_____ AMOUNT

16
I will write from
_____ TIME
_____ AM/PM
to
_____ TIME
_____ AM/PM
Word-count goal for the day
_____ AMOUNT

17
I will write from
_____ TIME
_____ AM/PM
to
_____ TIME
_____ AM/PM
Word-count goal for the day
_____ AMOUNT

18
I will write from
_____ TIME
_____ AM/PM
to
_____ TIME
_____ AM/PM
Word-count goal for the day
_____ AMOUNT

19
I will write from
_____ TIME
_____ AM/PM
to
_____ TIME
_____ AM/PM
Word-count goal for the day
_____ AMOUNT

20
I will write from
_____ TIME
_____ AM/PM
to
_____ TIME
_____ AM/PM
Word-count goal for the day
_____ AMOUNT

21
I will write from
_____ TIME
_____ AM/PM
to
_____ TIME
_____ AM/PM
Word-count goal for the day
_____ AMOUNT

22
I will write from
_____ TIME
_____ AM/PM
to
_____ TIME
_____ AM/PM
Word-count goal for the day
_____ AMOUNT

23
I will write from
_____ TIME
_____ AM/PM
to
_____ TIME
_____ AM/PM
Word-count goal for the day
_____ AMOUNT

24
I will write from
_____ TIME
_____ AM/PM
to
_____ TIME
_____ AM/PM
Word-count goal for the day
_____ AMOUNT

25
I will write from
_____ TIME
_____ AM/PM
to
_____ TIME
_____ AM/PM
Word-count goal for the day
_____ AMOUNT

26
I will write from
_____ TIME
_____ AM/PM
to
_____ TIME
_____ AM/PM
Word-count goal for the day
_____ AMOUNT

27
I will write from
_____ TIME
_____ AM/PM
to
_____ TIME
_____ AM/PM
Word-count goal for the day
_____ AMOUNT

28
I will write from
_____ TIME
_____ AM/PM
to
_____ TIME
_____ AM/PM
Word-count goal for the day
_____ AMOUNT

29
I will write from
_____ TIME
_____ AM/PM
to
_____ TIME
_____ AM/PM
Word-count goal for the day
_____ AMOUNT

30
I will write from
_____ TIME
_____ AM/PM
to
_____ TIME
_____ AM/PM
Word-count goal for the day
_____ AMOUNT

Ready, Set, Write . . . And Keep Writing!

NaNoWriMo's Personal Chart of Noveling Progress

Write your word-count goal at the top of this page, and color this chart in as you make progress on your novel. To find out what each milestone should be, divide your total word-count goal by 10. This number will be the amount of words you have to write to reach the next milestone.

If your word-count goal is 5,000, you'll need to write 500 to reach the first milestone, then another 500 (or 1,000 total words) to reach the second milestone, and so on.

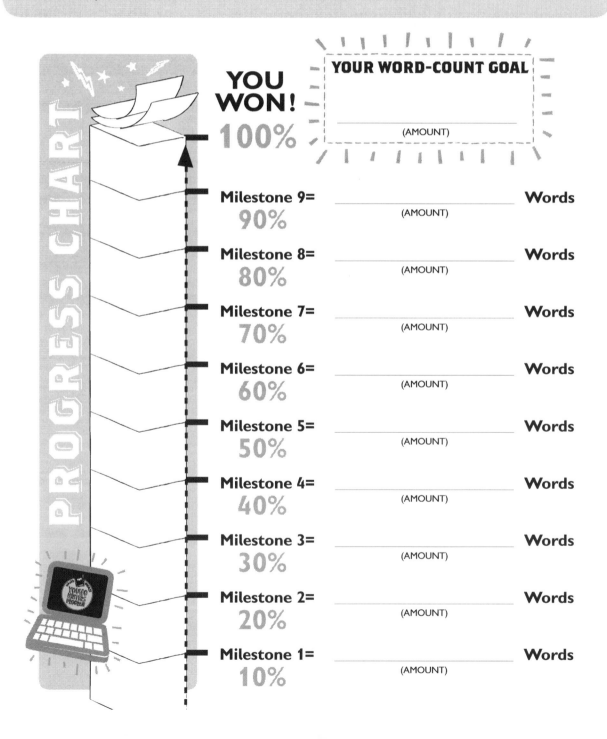

YOU WON!
100%

YOUR WORD-COUNT GOAL

_____
(AMOUNT)

Milestone 9= _____ **Words**
90% (AMOUNT)

Milestone 8= _____ **Words**
80% (AMOUNT)

Milestone 7= _____ **Words**
70% (AMOUNT)

Milestone 6= _____ **Words**
60% (AMOUNT)

Milestone 5= _____ **Words**
50% (AMOUNT)

Milestone 4= _____ **Words**
40% (AMOUNT)

Milestone 3= _____ **Words**
30% (AMOUNT)

Milestone 2= _____ **Words**
20% (AMOUNT)

Milestone 1= _____ **Words**
10% (AMOUNT)

PROGRESS CHART

Back to the Beginning!

Here you are, ready to start your novel! We know what you're thinking. You're thinking *"Okay, I've got my paper, my pencil, my lucky pencil sharpener, 15 packs of gum, a month's supply of energy drinks, and my noveling iPod playlist to get me pumped and ready to go. So now what?"*

If you are feeling a little nervous, and the blank page and you are having a staring contest, don't worry! It's perfectly natural. Many novelists will tell you that figuring out the first few lines of a novel is the hardest part. Lucky for you, you're about a million steps ahead of most novelists—you've already got your characters, your plot, your setting, *and* you know how to write some seriously awesome dialogue! Not bad for a month's work.

Like we said earlier, there are several ways to start your novel. You can begin with the inciting incident or work backwards from the resolution to the beginning. Novels are filled with flashbacks, flash-forwards, and unexpected plot twists. So feel free to begin anywhere you like!

You can:

- Start at the beginning.

- Start at your inciting incident.

- Start *in medias res* (in the middle of things).

- Start at the end.

Start at the Beginning

As you learned in the "Outlining Your Plot" worksheet, the beginning or set-up of your novel needs to introduce your characters and your conflict. Starting a novel at the very beginning is a great way to ease your readers in. So many stories and fairy tales begin this way (Once upon a time...), that readers feel right at home in your story almost immediately.

> There once lived a young girl named Judy who spent almost every moment of every day dreaming about owning her very own horse. And to her surprise, on the morning of her fourteenth birthday, a genie popped out of her box of cornflakes. His name was Bob, and he smelled slightly of onions. But that was okay—she was finally going to get the horse she'd always wanted.

Try starting your novel at the beginning. Take out your plot worksheet and review your set-up. Make sure you include your protagonist in your beginning, and you may also want to introduce your main conflict, and a supporting character.

Start with the Inciting Incident

The inciting incident, as you know, is the moment that changes your protagonist's life and launches them into his/her adventure. Starting with this moment sucks your readers into your story, and leaves them wondering what will happen next.

> Two days after Judy's fourteenth birthday, she woke up to find that she had turned into a horse. This was not what she wished for. She should've known not to trust a genie with a name like Bob.

Now try and begin with the inciting incident. Go back and review your inciting incident and then write a beginning to your novel that starts with this event.

_____

_____

_____

_____

_____

_____

_____

_____

Start *In Medias Res*

In medias res (pronounced *en med-ee-ya rez*) is Latin for "in the middle of things." It literally means starting your story right smack in the middle of the action, and then filling in the holes—explaining who the characters are and what got them into the mess they're in. A lot of suspense, mystery, and action novels begin *in medias res*. It's a great way to draw readers in and to make sure they stick around for all the details.

> Judy stood standing face to face with the four-headed dragon from the planet Gandoria—its eyes spinning with rage and spit pooling at the corners of its hungry mouths. She couldn't help but wonder how she got here, and more importantly, where Bob was.

Start *in medias res*. Check out your rising action, falling action, and climax to see if there are any moments you might want to start with.

_____

_____

_____

_____

_____

_____

_____

_____

_____

Start at the End

This one is a bit tricky, but well worth a try! You basically tell the ending to your readers, but leave just enough mystery to keep them reading. Then, you can either work backwards to reveal just how that ending came about or jump to any other point of your novel and continue.

> When it was all over and Judy was finally the queen of that forsaken land, she looked back and knew that it had all been worth it. She had learned to love Bob even if he did smell like onions, and knew that she would never want to be anything else but the horse she had become.

Start at the end. Try to include clues to the story's main conflict so readers get some idea of what the rest of the novel will be about and intrigue them to learn more.

_____

_____

_____

_____

_____

_____

_____

_____

Now you have a bunch of beginnings to start with. Recopy your favorite in your noveling notebook or onto your computer, and write, write, write!

Details, Details, Details

The noveling has begun, and you've been writing like a mad person. If your word count is looking pathetic, we have a solution. The number one way to get your word count soaring and give your readers descriptions they'll never forget is by adding concrete and sensory details to your novel.

Concrete details are those details in your novel that come right out of your five senses:

 1. Taste

 2. Touch

 3. Smell

 4. Sight

 5. Hearing

"There was a dog in the alley." = 7 words

"There was a wet, one-eyed beagle covered in black mud, smelling like the inside of a sewage drainpipe in the alley next to the deserted bus station." = 27 words

Below, we've listed a few things that could use some spicing up in the detail department. We've also provided you with some cool Word Banks with very impressive synonyms. In the spaces provided, answer the questions for each of the following items, using your senses and our Word Banks to make your descriptions come alive on the page.

A thunderstorm

What does it feel like?

_____

_____

_____

_____

_____

_____

What does it smell like?

_____

_____

_____

_____

What do the clouds look like? What does the rain gathering in the streets look like?

_____

_____

_____

_____

What does it sound like?

_____

_____

_____

_____

_____

What does the rain taste like?

_____

_____

_____

_____

_____

_____

A rock concert

What does it feel like?

_____

_____

_____

_____

_____

What does it smell like?

_____

_____

_____

_____

_____

What do you see?

_____

_____

Word Bank for "Interesting"

captivating,
compelling,
entertaining,
stimulating,
intriguing,
fascinating,
absorbing,
engaging,
enchanting,
challenging,
attractive,
gripping,
riveting,
enthralling,
exhilarating,
mesmerizing,
noteworthy,
striking,
significant

_____

_____

_____

Word Bank for "Funny"

hilarious, comical, humorous, weird, curious, droll, absurd, ridiculous, silly, witty, side-splitting, laughable, odd, peculiar, ludicrous, riotous, hysterical, uproarious, slapstick, zany

What does it sound like?

_____

_____

_____

_____

_____

An abandoned house

How does it make you feel?

_____

_____

_____

_____

_____

What does it smell like?

_____

_____

_____

_____

_____

What do you see inside?

_____

_____

_____

_____

_____

_____

What do you hear?

_____

_____

_____

_____

_____

_____

_____

Bonus Exercise: The NaNoWriMo Description Challenge

The following things are a little more difficult to describe, but not impossible. If you can describe the following using all your senses, you will have no problem reaching your word count this November.

A blank white wall

Taste:

_____

_____

_____

_____

_____

Touch:

_____

_____

_____

_____

_____

Smell:

_____

_____

_____

_____

_____

Sight:

_____

_____

_____

_____

_____

Sound:

_____

> **Word Bank for "Good"**
>
> excellent,
> superior,
> outstanding,
> tremendous,
> fantastic, terrific,
> exemplary,
> desirable,
> beneficial,
> advantageous,
> favorable, decent,
> superlative,
> proficient,
> marvelous, useful,
> exceptional,
> incredible,
> altruistic, angelic

_____

_____

_____

_____

_____

Embarrassment

Taste:

_____

_____

_____

_____

Touch:

_____

_____

_____

_____

_____

Smell:

_____

_____

_____

_____

> **Word Bank for "Evil"**
>
> deplorable, malevolent, wicked, immoral, depraved, corrupt, degenerate, diabolical, heinous, sinister, sinful, reprobate, monstrous, fiendish, infernal, demonic, malicious, hateful, iniquitous, nefarious

Sight:

_____

_____

_____

_____

_____

Sound:

_____

_____

_____

_____

Word Bank for "Fun"

amusing, enjoyable, pleasurable, festive, recreational, exciting, playful, merry, entertaining, appealing, mirthful, jovial, cheerful, celebratory, jollity, convivial, gay, jocular, animated, gleeful

Happiness

Taste:

_____

_____

_____

_____

Touch:

_____

_____

_____

_____

_____

_____

Smell:

_____

_____

_____

_____

_____

Sight:

_____

_____

_____

_____

_____

Sound:

_____

_____

_____

_____

_____

Word Bank for "Awesome"

breathtaking, amazing, remarkable, extraordinary, outstanding, incredible, magnificent, wonderful, superb, fantastic, grand, astonishing, majestic, notable, phenomenal, stupendous, spectacular, unparalleled, supreme, striking

The universe!

Taste:

_____

_____

_____

_____

_____

_____

Touch:

_____

_____

_____

_____

_____

_____

Smell:

_____

_____

_____

_____

_____

_____

Sight:

_____

_____

_____

_____

_____

_____

Sound:

_____

_____

_____

_____

Does your brain hurt? We thought it might. Try and describe that!

Your hurting brain

Taste:

_____

_____

_____

_____

Touch:

_____

_____

_____

_____

_____

_____

Smell:

_____

_____

_____

_____

_____

Sight:

_____

_____

_____

_____

_____

Sound:

_____

_____

_____

_____

_____

Stupendous job! If you ever feel like your word count is waning, be sure to use your senses and add a lot of concrete and sensory details.

Sub-Plotting

The More Plots, the Merrier

A sure-fire way to guarantee that there is enough action in your novel to fill the pages, meet your word count, and keep your readers reading is to add subplots starring your supporting characters. Just like your protagonist and antagonist, your supporting characters have dreams, fears, and weaknesses of their own.

> If your protagonist wants to travel to Chicago for the freestyle hip-hop competitions to fulfill his dream of becoming a performer, perhaps his best friend wants to become a chef and is coming along for Chicago's world-famous, five-star restaurants.

Since you may have more than one supporting character, complete the following for each of them on a separate sheet of paper:

More than anything in the world, _____ wants:

Supporting character's name

But he/she is afraid of:

And his/her greatest weakness is:

Watching TV is a great way to learn about subplots. Shows like *The Simpsons* are filled with them. Episodes aren't always about Homer or Bart. Lisa, Marge, and even Maggie have adventures of their own that weave in and out of the main plot line. For this reason, we would like you to take a break from noveling and watch some TV. Don't get too excited though. You're not totally off the hook . . .

You have to choose a fictional show—meaning no reality-TV shows—and it can't be a show you really like. Otherwise, you will get too lost in the episode to pay attention to the assignment. Which is to sit down in front of the tube, put your thinking cap on, and write down answers to the following questions in your notebook:

1. Who is the protagonist?

2. How many supporting characters are there? Who are they? And how are they related to the protagonist?

3. What are the subplots? These are the plots that involve the supporting characters going after something they want. They may include the protagonist, but sometimes the protagonist has little to no connection to the subplot.

4. Do the supporting characters have their own antagonists? Or are they also battling the protagonist's antagonist?

As you probably noticed, within the main plot of the show, the writers have inserted several minor plots involving the supporting characters. Now that you know about your supporting characters' hopes and fears, you can add subplots to your own story.

Anytime you feel stuck or bored with your protagonist, go see what your supporting characters are up to. You can totally switch gears and follow their journeys whenever you'd like. Maybe they'll run into your protagonist, maybe they won't. No matter what happens, we promise that all kinds of unexpected things will unfold each time you explore a subplot.

Character Interviews on NaNo-TV

One of the best ways to *really* get to know your characters is to step inside their shoes for a little while, that is, to pretend that you are your characters! And guess what? We've given you the perfect opportunity to do just that, because your characters have been invited to be interviewed on the local NaNo-TV station.

With a friend or by yourself, answer the interview questions as your characters would answer them. If it helps you to get into the roles before you start, try closing your eyes and imagining how your characters speak and move. Maybe slink around the room like your protagonist would, or talk in a French accent if your supporting character is French.

PROTAGONIST INTERVIEW

Host: Hello, _____ , and welcome to *NaNo-TV*, the best TV-show ever.
                    (your protagonist's name),
We're really excited about _____ novel, and are honored to have you
                                         (your name)'s
on the show. Why don't you tell us a little about your journey so far? What exactly are you setting out to achieve?

Protagonist:

_____

_____

_____

_____

_____

Host: Wow! Sounds like quite a goal. Rumor has it, though, that someone is out to get you. We've heard you've been having some trouble with a particular antagonist. Can you tell us a little about what this person has been up to lately?

Protagonist:

_____

_____

_____

_____

_____

_____

Host: Man, sounds pretty wild! Now, we all know that you are a fictional character, but we've heard that you have quite a mind of your own. Have you done anything unexpected this November to surprise the person writing about you?

Protagonist:

_____

_____

_____

_____

_____

_____

Host: Real quick, a question that's been weighing on everyone's minds—What would you rather do: live without music or live without TV? Why?

Protagonist:

_____

_____

_____

_____

_____

_____

Host: How do you feel now about the rest of your adventure? Is there anything you're anxious about?

_____

_____

_____

Host: Well, we wish you the best of luck! We're confident you will succeed! Do you have any secret plans for defeating your antagonist?

Protagonist:

_____

_____

_____

_____

_____

Okay, now it's time for one of your supporting characters to be interviewed! Choose your favorite supporting character, or one you want to get to know better, and take a few minutes to get into character.

SUPPORTING CHARACTER INTERVIEW

Host: Hello, _____ , and welcome to the show! We just talked
            (your supporting character's name)
to _____ and learned all about _____ . We
     (your protagonist's name)   (your antagonist's name)
just heard about the protagonist's plans for defeating the antagonist. Do you have any other tricks up your sleeve that we don't know about?

Supporting Character:

_____

_____

_____

_____

_____

Host: Wow, tricky indeed. What special challenges have you faced while helping the protagonist?

Supporting Character:

_____

_____

_____

_____

_____

Host: We all know that you've been a big help to the protagonist, but we're also wondering: Is there anything or anyone that's been a big help to you along the way?

Supporting Character:

_____

_____

_____

_____

_____

Host: Very interesting. Hey, it looks like we've got a call coming through. Hello, you're on _NaNo-TV_, the best TV show ever. What's your question?

Caller: Yes, hi. Wow, I've never called into a TV-show before! Hi Mom! Anyway, my question is: If you could only three foods for the rest of your life, what three foods would you choose?

Supporting Character:

_____

_____

_____

_____

Host: Good answer. Moving on, is there anything in particular that you're excited or nervous about for the upcoming adventures you face?

Supporting Character:

_____

_____

_____

_____

_____

Host: Well, we wish you all the best of luck in supporting _____ , and

                                                   (protagonist)

we look forward to hearing how things pan out for you. One last thing, before you go: What do you plan on doing after this novel is over?

Supporting Character:

_____

_____

_____

_____

_____

Host: Wow! Wish I could join you! Thank you so much for your time. We hope you'll join us again soon. Up next, the character you've all been waiting for... the antagonist, just after this commercial break!

All right, now it's time to get antagonistic! Whatever you need to do, take a few minutes to get into character—then, let your antagonist take center stage.

ANTAGONIST INTERVIEW

Host: Hi, _____ , and welcome to the show! Why don't you tell us a
              (your antagonist's name)
little about yourself? Like, what has made you so unpleasant?

Antagonist:

_____

_____

_____

_____

_____

_____

Host: I can see why your reputation precedes you. We've just spoken to

_____ and _____ , and they've told us
   (your protagonist's name)   (your supporting character's name)
a little about the conflict you all are having. Would you like to give your side of the story?

Antagonist:

_____

_____

_____

_____

_____

Host: Fascinating. Is there a certain reason why you and the protagonist are enemies? Were you ever friends?

Antagonist:

_____

_____

Host: Is there anything you plan to do in the novel that you haven't done so far? Any nasty tricks up your sleeve you'd like to tell us about?

Antagonist:

_____

_____

_____

Host: That is _messed up_! You really are an antagonist, in every way. Oh, it looks like we've got another call coming through! Caller, welcome to the show. What's your question?

Caller: _Yes, hello. I'm a research scientist and I'm doing a study on antagonists. I was wondering if there are any ways in which things might be different if this was your novel, instead of the protagonist's?_

Antagonist:

_____

_____

_____

_____

Host: Fascinating. It looks like we're running out of time. Well, antagonist, we can't say we wish you luck, but we do look forward to hearing how things turn out. We hope you'll come back again and join us when November is over. And to all our viewers out there in TV land, be sure to join us tomorrow, when I'll be arm wrestling a ravenous koala bear, blind-folded. See you then!

Bonus Challenge!

If you are doing this with a friend, and you two are having a good time interviewing and getting interviewed, keep going! Make up your own questions to ask each other, and do interviews as all your supporting characters.

Lists, Lists, and Lists of Lists

"During the month of November, Abigail was busy with all kinds of activities. Not only was she writing a novel in a month (no easy feat!), but she was also training for a marathon, planning a cook-out for her boyfriend Boris, learning to knit, and opening her very own yoga studio. Plus, she was really busy with all kinds of world-changing activities, like writing daily postcards to the White House calling for more fuel-efficient energy and better recycling programs."

Oh hey, we were just doing one of our favorite noveling activities—taking the items from a list we made called "All the important things Abigail does in November."

Lists are great because they do a lot of things at once:

1. They help us discover new things about our characters.
2. They reveal plot twists.
2. They help boost word counts (always a plus!).

You can use the suggested list topics below in many different ways. Here are a some ideas:

1. You can fill out the lists in the spaces below to see if you discover anything new about your characters or plot that will take your novel in a new direction.
2. You can take the items from your lists and write them into your novel as full sentences just like we've done in the example above.
3. You can just read the list of suggested lists below and see if any of them spur new ideas and write from there.

Whichever way you choose to do it, make sure to let your brain loose and just write. If you run out of room in any given box, take out a separate sheet of paper and keep writing!

Protagonist Lists

Hidden things in your protagonist's room:

_____

_____

_____

_____

_____

_____

_____

Things in your protagonist's refrigerator and freezer:

_____

_____

_____

_____

_____

_____

_____

Your protagonist's bad habits:

_____

_____

_____

_____

_____

_____

_____

What your protagonist daydreams about:

_____

_____

_____

_____

_____

_____

_____

Antagonist Lists

Things in your antagonist's closet:

_____

_____

_____

_____

_____

_____

_____

_____

Things your antagonist collects:

_____

_____

_____

_____

_____

_____

_____

_____

Things your antagonist carries in his/her pockets or bag:

_____

_____

_____

_____

_____

_____

Jobs your antagonist had before ending up in your novel:

_____

_____

_____

_____

_____

_____

Bonus Exercise

If you like lists and you finish with these, come up with your own list of lists. Anytime you get stuck during NaNoWriMo, take out your list of lists and get writing. A list prompt like "Things my protagonist wants to eat this very moment" may help you get out of a rut and get your story moving again. . . to the taco truck!

I Wrote a Novel!
Now What?

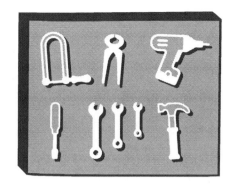

The Workshop

Today is a great day for your novel, because today your novel will be read for the very first time by another living, breathing person! Fortunately, that person is also a novelist. He or she knows exactly what you've been through in the last month and will have a lot of useful insight into your work. Unfortunately, this does not mean your work is finished. Your fellow novelist will have questions, comments, and maybe even complaints about what you've written so far. You'll need to consider these and make decisions about what to change.

Below are guidelines you and this fellow novelist—your workshop partner—will follow as you read one another's novels. You may want to add a few of your own guidelines to the list.

- **Read through your partner's draft once without writing comments.** This can be a quick skim to get an idea of what the story is about and who some of the characters are. Then read it again more carefully.

- **Forget about grammar, spelling, and how you would say something if it were your novel.** Today, focus on the content of the story—the characters, the events, the setting, the awesome writing tricks your partner used!

- **Take time to circle words, sentences, or whole sections that you really like.** Then, in the margins, write a word or two to tell what you liked about each one.

- **Ask lot of questions.** If something doesn't make sense, ask about it. If you need more detail about a character, ask about it. If you just want to know how your partner came up with a word, phrase, or idea, ask about it!

- **Be kind—and specific—as you point out things that just aren't "working."** "I lost interest by the end of this paragraph because it's so long" is much more constructive than "I don't like this paragraph."

- **Keep the criticism between you and your partner.** No one else needs to hear how you thought so-and-so's first sentence was super-boring!

To get a clearer idea of what "helpful" feedback looks like, compare these two paragraphs.

Not So Helpful

"Stop, thief!" Eloise cried. People on the street stared as the guy took off with her precious backpack. Eloise panicked. She had to get that pack back! What would she tell Juan when she arrived at their secret meeting spot without it? And how would they transform him from a clumsy, shy dancer into a spinning, jumping disco freak in time for their competition without the special dance-o-meter that was inside?

> This sentence is a little boring

> ??

> I like your writing.

The main problem with these comments is that, like a dull novel, they lack detail. The first comment does not give specifics about why that sentence might be boring. And the last comment, "I like your writing," doesn't let the writer know what he/she is specifically doing well. Now check out the comments below.

More Helpful

"Stop, thief!" Eloise cried. People on the street stared as the guy took off with her precious backpack. Eloise panicked. She had to get that pack back! What would she tell Juan when she arrived at their secret meeting spot without it? And how would they transform him from a clumsy, shy dancer into a spinning, jumping disco freak in time for their competition without the special dance-o-meter that was inside?

> Add detail here. What did the guy look like? What were the people doing as they stared? Etc.

> Did you rhyme on purpose? Nice!

> I love your use of suspense. I want to read more!

The comments here are more helpful because they are more specific. Now the writer knows what he or she needs to revise, as well as what he or she is already doing well.

Reader Review Worksheet

Take out your workshop partner's draft and fill in the blanks below. And remember, be specific! Return this sheet to your partner when you are done.

Your workshop partner's name:

_____

Novel Title: _____

1. Based on the beginning, what do you think this novel is about?

_____

_____

_____

_____

2. Who is the most important character so far? What is he or she like?

_____

_____

_____

_____

3. What do you like most about your partner's first line and paragraph?

_____

_____

_____

_____

4. What is the setting? What other details would you like to know about it?

_____

_____

_____

5. List three things you really like about your partner's work so far.

_____

_____

_____

_____

_____

_____

6. List three things your partner can work on as he or she revises.

_____

_____

_____

_____

_____

_____

Unleash Your Inner Editor

Your Inner Editor is *almost* ready to get to work. You've gotten some helpful editing notes from classmates—which is a great start—but your classmates were not able to read your entire novel. Revising your whole book might seem pretty overwhelming at first, but this worksheet will help you make a manageable and realistic revision plan!

You'll want to start by recalling all the hopes and dreams you had as you wrote your first draft. What was your goal in writing? Another way to think about this is to ask yourself what you hope readers will think or feel after reading your novel.

> **Here are some example goals:**
>
> "I want to move people to care more about the Earth's environment."
>
> "I want to help people understand that sea monkeys totally should be allowed to fly airplanes."
>
> "I want to show that love really does conquer all."
>
> "I want to make people laugh until they cry."
>
> "I want to show that winning the lottery isn't everything!"

Write your goal below, using a complete sentence.

My Goal:

_____

_____

_____

_____

_____

Now use the novel draft you've got with you, as well as your own recollections from writing, to fill out each section below. And keep that goal you wrote on the last page in mind; it will help keep you focused when you start to feel overwhelmed by details.

Note: You may notice that none of the questions below have to do with grammar or typos. You and your Inner Editor will do that absolutely last, after you've revised your novel in every other way.

I. Organization

1. Is your novel organized in chapters? If so, how did you decide where to make chapter breaks? If you didn't use chapters, why not?

_____

_____

_____

_____

2. Find and read a few transitions between chapters and/or between settings/scenes. Describe some transitions—or links—you created between chapters and/or events to make the organization clear.

_____

_____

_____

_____

_____

3. Name three places in your novel where readers might get confused about the order of events.

- _____

- _____

- _____

4. Name three changes you plan to make as you re-organize your novel. These changes could be big (moving whole chapters) or small (adding transition words like "then" to make the flow of events or ideas clearer).

- _____

- _____

- _____

II. Voice and Writing Style

1. How would you describe your writing style? Tell how the words and sentences in your novel might sound if read aloud (such as dramatic, dark, simple, minimalistic, stark, dry, funny and light hearted, wordy and highly intellectual, etc.).

_____

_____

_____

_____

_____

_____

2. Open your novel to any page. Skim the paragraphs. Do they sound like they were all written in the same voice? If not, why not?

_____

_____

_____

_____

3. Name three changes you plan to make as you revise the voice and writing style of your novel. These changes could be big (getting rid of jokes throughout) or small (trying not to use the word "totally" so much).

- _____

- _____

- _____

III. Plot and Conflict

1. In three sentences or less, describe the plot of your novel.

_____

_____

_____

_____

_____

2. In one sentence, describe the conflict in your novel.

_____

_____

_____

_____

_____

3. Open your novel to one page, any page. (If you turn to a page related to your subplot, try again.) Skim the paragraphs. Then repeat with another page. Did you or your characters lose focus on your main plot or conflict at any point? Is this okay, or do you think readers might get confused?

_____

_____

_____

_____

_____

4. Name three changes you plan to make so your novel's plot and conflict are clearer.

- _____

- _____

- _____

IV. Literary Features that Make Your Novel Fun to Read

Which of the following special features did you use a lot of in your novel? First complete the lists below with features you like to see in novels, such as suspense or humor. Then check off all the listed items *you* used and *did not* use.

1. I used:

☐ Dialogue that shows without telling

☐ Sensory detail about settings

☐ Sensory detail about characters

☐ Plot twists

☐ Suspense

☐ Other: _____

☐ Other: _____

☐ Other: _____

☐ Other: _____

☐ Other: _____

2. Open your novel to one page, any page. Skim the paragraphs. Then repeat. Which of the following did you *not* use so much:

☐ Dialogue that shows without telling

☐ Sensory detail about settings

☐ Sensory detail about characters

☐ Plot twists

☐ Suspense

☐ Other: _____

☐ Other: _____

☐ Other: _____

☐ Other: _____

☐ Other: _____

3. Name three ways you plan to revise your novel to improve the dialogue, sensory detail, subplots, or any of the other features you listed above. These changes could be big (add dialogue everywhere) or small (add more sensory details to the car chase on page 10).

- _____

- _____

- _____

OK, now you have a plan for revising your novel. Let that Inner Editor loose!

Cleaning It Up

All month long, we've told you to focus on getting your words on paper. "Don't worry if it's not perfect," we've repeated. "Write as much as possible," we've reminded. Now we take it all back! Well, not really, but here's the deal: You've worked really hard on this novel, and while it doesn't have to be perfect, you also don't want it to be full of typos. Typos and grammar mistakes really distract readers' attention away from your brilliant story. And who knows what you may do with this novel in future? Maybe you'll want to submit it to a contest. Maybe you'll want to try to get it published. If so, you're going to have to do the dreaded deed anyway: proofread.

Below are a few areas where writing can get messy. Read the description of each writing woe then grab your very best red pen, imagine it's a scrub-brush, and clean up the messy sentences

Tricksters
First, check your spelling. But don't think you can count on your computer's spell check. Spell check won't pick up on tricky words that sound alike, such as *they're, their, and there*. You've got to use your own brain to find those mistakes!

> The excitement was sew grate that Heidi couldn't bear it. They're was know way to describe the intents anticipation.

From Beginning to End
Yes, we're going to remind you. Use correct capitalization and punctuation, including commas, semicolons, quotation marks, parentheses, dashes and end marks. Your reader will get lost if you don't follow the basic rules.

> the crowded stadium went silent her older brother matt grabbed the bat stepping up to the base he looked so grown-up in his los angeles uniform?

Make Your Mark!

∧	insert
ϐ	delete
∽	switch
⊙	period
⋏	comma
⅋	quotation marks
¶	start new paragraph

Pick and Stick

It is important to stay with one verb tense. There are times when you may have to switch (dialogue, flashbacks) but for the most part, pick a tense and stick to it.

> The summer evening was filled with cheers and suddenly, the crack of a bat. Heidi closes her eyes for a minute and tries to imagine the ball heading way, way out of the stadium.

We Agree

Make sure all your subjects and verbs agree.

> The people in the seats in front of her started to jump up and down. Matt had hit a homerun!

In Good Form

Make sure to choose the correct form of every pronoun.

> Her was feeling as giddy as a child on they first day of school.

Keep It Active

Make sure every sentence has a clear subject that the reader can easily visualize. Avoid using feelings or ideas as subjects; use characters instead. This is called using the "active voice."

> The pride was overwhelming Heidi as it swept over her and her mother sitting next to her. The excitement felt by Matt was intense and in slow motion as he ran.

Mix It Up!

Have you ever heard the phrase "variety is the spice of life"? It's true for sentences, too. Keep your writing interesting by using different sentence lengths and types.

> The crowd cheered wildly. Heidi felt it. It felt like a heart beat. It felt like it was inside her.

Now take a look at the beginning of a novel below. It's got promise, but it's also got some major problems. Wield thy mighty red pen!

James Frederick Monroe, why are you late?

Jim looked directly down at the floor. How could him answer that question without being sentenced to a year of house arrest. His mother had bald him out last week just for forgetting to take out the trash garbage. This was way worst than that. Jim knew it isn't his fault that he is late. but the reason was to risky to confess. Just then a lie presented itself to he. "It all began with Tommy" Jim said after takeing a slow, deep breathe.

Now it's really time to unleash that Inner Editor of yours. Apply this checklist to your own novel!

☐ Every sentence and proper noun begins with a capital letter.

☐ Every sentence has the correct end mark.

☐ I use other punctuation marks such as commas, semicolons, and quotation marks correctly.

☐ I use commas, dashes, or parentheses to separate ideas within a sentence when necessary

☐ I use a variety of sentences types and lengths.

☐ I use a consistent verb tense.

☐ All my subjects and verbs agree.

☐ I use the correct form of every pronoun.

☐ All my sentences are active.

☐ I have checked my spelling.

☐ I have *really* checked my spelling and looked for tricky words!

After you check off all of the following, and you feel confident about your manuscript, go to the "Resources" section on the NaNoWriMo YWP site (http://ywp.nanowrimo.org) for opportunities to publish your book, submit to contests, and continue your brilliant writing career!

Choosing an Exceptional Excerpt

Congratulations on completing your novel! Hopefully, you've read your manuscript plenty of times while editing and rewriting. Now it's time to let others in on your hard work.

The Bad News: Most literary publications that print student writing aren't able to include your whole novel. Can you imagine if they got a manuscript from every middle schooler who wrote for NaNoWriMo? They would be overwhelmed!

The Good News: Those same publications are very willing and excited to publish excerpts—short sections—from your novel. This worksheet is a guide for how to pick the best excerpts to submit and—fingers crossed—get published. (If you're still bummed about the bad news, talk to your teacher or check the NaNoWriMo website for resources to self-publish or submit your entire manuscript.)

A good excerpt represents your novel at its best. It should be short but engaging; in the best case, it makes the reader want to know more about your plot and characters. Here are some of the traits of an excerpt that really **CALLS** out to publishers and readers:

Character - Remember that readers are most interested in original, well-developed characters. They want people they can love, hate, relate to, and so on. So be sure your excerpt includes a strong sense of at least one important character.

Action - Choose a part of your story where something important, crazy, mysterious, sad, or funny happens. In other words, think about an event in your novel that really stands out. Chances are it will also stand out in an excerpt!

Language - You've worked hard on the language in your novel. You've crafted great dialogue and description, and used imagery, metaphors, and similes to put pictures in the reader's mind. What part makes you say, "Wow, I love my language here"?

Length - A good, publishable length for an excerpt is generally about 1,000 words (2 pages, if your manuscript is double-spaced). Don't worry if you go over or under a little.

Stands on Its Own - Readers may be confused if you choose an excerpt that doesn't make sense without knowing the rest of the story, or a part with too much description. Think of the excerpt as a mini-novel, with a clear beginning, middle, and end.

Use the space below to name a few sections or chapters that might make good excerpts. List three different options, including page numbers for where each excerpt starts and ends. What makes each excerpt exceptional? Explain in your notes.

* _____

_____

_____

_____

_____

* _____

_____

_____

_____

_____

* _____

_____

_____

_____

Writing a Superior Submission Letter

Next, you need to give the editors who will read your writing some background information about what you're sending. Do this by writing a good "submission letter." **A submission letter is a brief note to an editor giving him or her an idea of who you are and what your work is about.**

Think about the important parts of a good submission letter, described below. If you have ever written a formal letter, some of these will already be familiar to you! (We've also set this section up as a checklist so that as you write your own letter, you can check to make sure you've included each section.)

☐ **Heading** - This is where you give your name, home or school address, and the date you're sending the letter. (Ask your teacher for a model of how to format these if you're unfamiliar with standard letter writing.) Also include your phone number or e-mail address; this is often the easiest way for editors to contact you.

☐ **Greeting** - "Official" letters don't start with "Dear So-and-So," as you might normally write to your aunt or grandmother. Instead, they simply say the editor's name—"Mr. Jones," "Ms. Jefferson," etc.—with a colon at the end. If you can't find the editor's name, you can use "To Whom It May Concern."

☐ **Background Info** - Tell the editor your name, age, school, and any other information he or she may want to know. You might want to mention NaNoWriMo, too, since many publishers who print student writing will be familiar with it.

☐ **Novel Info** - Provide the editor with a brief description of your novel. It shouldn't be too detailed—about two or three sentences at most. You may have already done this before you started editing! Check page 93 in your workbook.

☐ **Request** - Here's where you say why you're writing. State very clearly that you are including an excerpt to possibly be printed. Most editors will know the reason for your letter, but it doesn't hurt to be obvious.

☐ **Closing** - Politely remind the editor why you've written, and be sure to say thanks for his or her time. This can go a long way! Sign your letter with "Sincerely" and your name.

Now take a look at the parts of a superior submission letter in action:

Heading

Sammy Student
3354 Adeline St.
Berkeley, CA 94703
sammy.student@gmail.com

November 30, 2010

Greeting

To Whom It May Concern:

Background Info

My name is Sammy Student. I am a seventh grader at Martin Luther King, Jr. Middle School in Berkeley, CA. This November, my class participated in National Novel Writing Month, an event where students write their own novels.

Novel Info

I wrote a novel called Zombie Dog. It is about a fat Chihuahua named Buster who gets bit by another dog and turns into a zombie. Buster is afraid his owner Hannah will not want to keep him if she finds out he is a zombie. One day, though, he cannot hide it anymore. That's when the story gets really crazy!

Request

I am submitting an excerpt from Zombie Dog to be included in Fantasy Journal. The excerpt is about 1,200 words. Please consider printing my excerpt in your journal. Thanks for your time.

Closing

Sincerely,
Sammy Student

It's finally your turn! Draft your letter below using the checklist on page 101. You can even lay that sheet, or the example letter, right next to this one if it helps you remember what to write.

_____

_____

_____

_____

_____

_____

_____

_____

_____

_____

_____

_____

_____

_____

_____

_____

Terrific. Now your first draft is complete. You're ready to make any little edits and proofread it—you remember how to do all that, right?—pop it in a stamped envelope with your excerpt, and voila! You're on your way to publishing success!

Made in the USA
Lexington, KY
21 May 2017